C000165355

My Favourite

Quotes &
Anecdotes

My Favourite

Quotes & Anecdotes

Selwyn Hughes

My Favourite Quotes and Anecdotes
compiled by Selwyn Hughes

Copyright © Selwyn Hughes 2001

Published by CWR, Waverley Abbey House, Waverley Lane, Farnham, Surrey, GU9 8EP.

ISBN 1-85345-196-7

All rights reserved. No part of this publication may be reproduced, stored in a retrieval system, or transmitted, in any form or by any means, electronic, mechanical, photocopying, recording or otherwise, without the prior permission of CWR.

All Scripture quotations in this publication are taken from the Holy Bible, New International Version (NIV). Copyright © 1973, 1978, 1984, International Bible Society. Used by permission.

This book is an edited compilation of quotes, anecdotes and stories collected by Selwyn Hughes during his 50 years in Christian ministry. Whilst every reasonable effort has been made to trace copyright holders, the publishers would be pleased to hear from any not acknowledged here. With special thanks to Robert Blackhouse, *5000 Quotations for Teachers and Preachers*, Kingsway Publications.

Concept development, editing, design and production by CWR. Cover image: Photodisc. Internal images: Eyewire.

Printed by Cox & Wyman

Contents

Introduction

After 50 years in Christian ministry I know how important it is to engage your congregation or reader, and the right quote or illustration can often help you make your point or explain an idea in an amusing and interesting way.

I hope that this little book helps you to communicate and have some fun. It might even take the hard work out of finding that much-needed quote to take from the dinner table to the pulpit.

Selwyn Hughes

Selwyn Hughes

The author's royalties from this series will be donated to a selection of Children's charities throughout the world.

1

Amusing Anecdotes and Quick Quotes

FAITH & CHURCH

An Individual INTERPRETATION

"What did you learn today?" a mother asked her little girl when she came home from Sunday School. "We learned the Lord's Prayer," came the response. "Wonderful. Can you remember how it begins?" her mother questioned. "Oh yes", the little girl replied, "Our Father in New Haven, how do you know my name?"

Member of the BOARD

At the end of a rather dull sermon, a newcomer to a church heard the preacher announce, "I would like to meet with the Official Board in the vestry when the service is over."

The newcomer turned to the person next to him and said, "If there is anyone more officially bored than I am, I would like to meet him."

A Sense of
OCCASION

An Anglican bishop in East Africa was asked to visit a village church to conduct a confirmation class for a couple, who also planned to marry.

As the church was over a hundred miles away from their home village, the bishop asked that arrangements be made for the couple first to be confirmed and then to be married all on the same day.

When he arrived at the village church he decided to change the order and perform the marriage service first and the confirmation second. The moment came when he asked the woman, "Will you take this man to be your lawful wedded husband?" Momentarily forgetful of the changed order of events, the young woman responded with great fervour, "I renounce the devil and all his works!"

Quick Quotes

"God rigs our world with situations that compel us to deal with those things that block us from being like Christ."
Larry Crabb

"The root of sin is the suspicion that God is not good."
Oswald Chambers

Preparing Your CONGREGATION

A long-winded American preacher heard criticism about his lengthy sermons. So, one Sunday he said, "Sorry if my sermons have been too long. Recently, I heard that the preamble to the Declaration of Independence contains 300 words, the Commandments 97 words, the Gettysburg Address 267 words, and The Lord's Prayer 100 words. However, a recent Government Report on the price of cabbages contains 26,911 words. Today's sermon will be somewhere

between the Lord's Prayer and the
cabbage report."

A CLERICAL *Error*

A rather old and doddery bishop attended a conference where he heard one of the speakers say, "The best years of my life were spent in the arms of another man's wife", meaning, of course, his mother. The bishop thought that would be a good statement with which to begin his sermon for Mothers' Day. A few weeks later, when Mothers' Day came round, he began his address from the pulpit by saying, "The best years of my life were spent in the arms of another man's wife but," he paused, "for the life of me I can't remember who she was."

POETIC *Preacher*

An old preacher, something of a poet, was feeling the effects of his age and put it like this in one of his sermons:

I've come to terms with my bi-focals,
To my deafness I'm resigned,
I've accepted my arthritis,
But, oh, how I miss my mind!

Quick Quotes

"The closer you get to God the less you understand Him but the more you trust Him."

"If God is calling you and you forget about it, just remember God won't."

Doctor Doctor

There were two doctors with the same name who lived a few doors apart. One was a Christian and a lay preacher, the other made no profession of faith.

One night, a rather sick person, also a Christian and wanting help from a fellow believer, knocked mistakenly at the door of the non-Christian doctor.

"Are you the doctor who preaches?" he asked. "No," the medic replied, "I am the doctor who practises." "Oh," said the sick person, "I've always understood the two things were inseparable."

Puppy TALE

A pastor confessed to his congregation one Sunday morning that he would have to be brief as his dog had eaten his sermon notes just before he left home. After the service, a visitor approached him and said, "If your dog ever has pups, I would like to buy one as a special gift to my pastor."

Wrong CONNECTION

A counsellor was given an opportunity to open a counselling office in a university. On the opening day, he sat at his desk for several hours before anyone came. Hearing someone enter the small waiting room, he picked up the phone and pretended he was talking to someone about their problems.

The man who had entered stood there silently, until the counsellor put down the phone and asked him how he could help. "I'm the telephone engineer," the man replied. "I've come to connect your phone."

Heavenly
INHERITANCE

In the days of Communist rule in Eastern Europe, when travel between countries was not as free as it is today, two Christians wanted to attend a secret gathering of believers in a nearby country.

At the border they said to the guard, "We are going to hear the last will and testament of our Elder Brother." They were let through. On their return the guard asked "How did it go?" "It went very well," they replied, "our Elder Brother left everything to us!"

Always NEAR

A pastor went to visit a dying member of his congregation. After he had spent some time talking to him and praying, he said, "I'm going to leave you now, but the Lord will be right here beside you. In fact, imagine Him sitting in the chair that I have been sitting in. Talk to Him and let Him whisper His comfort to your heart."

In the middle of the night the man died and, on his return the next day, the pastor asked the nurse who had attended him how he had died. "He died peacefully", the nurse replied, "but there was one curious thing – just before he

died he asked that I move the chair
alongside his bed closer to him. He
reached out his hand as if some unseen
hand were reaching out to him. Then, in
the most peaceful way, he died."

Quick Quotes

"Most of us read the Bible in the same way that a mouse tries to remove cheese from a trap. We just don't want to get caught."
Søren Kierkegaard

"I believe in Christianity as I believe the sun has risen, not because I see it but because by it I see everything else."
C S Lewis

A STICKY *Subject*

A little boy, lost, homeless and very hungry, found himself at a port where barrels of treacle were being unloaded from a ship into a warehouse on the quay.

As one of the cranes swung the barrels from ship to shore, the rope broke and one of the barrels fell and broke open at his feet. Seeing the treacle pouring out before him, the little boy lifted up his eyes to heaven and prayed, "Lord, oh for a tongue equal to the task!"

Treasured GUEST

Introducing a Christian speaker, a chairman began, "We have in our midst today someone whose name is a legend around the world. What a privilege it is to have him come to us and grace us with his presence."

The speaker, whose name was certainly not known world-wide, felt deeply troubled by this extravagant introduction and was about to protest modestly, when the chairman went on, "I'm referring, of course, to the Lord Jesus Christ, and here to tell us more about Him is one of His humble servants."

Quick Quotes

"Looking for Jesus in the Bible is like looking for David Jones in a Welsh telephone directory."
Eugene Peterson

"If people hate us because of Christ we are blessed; if they hate Christ because of us then we ought to get down on our knees and repent."

A TIMELY
Explanation

A young child attended an Anglican church service with his grandmother. As he had never been in an Anglican church before, she took care to explain the priest's every action as he conducted the service.

When the time came for the sermon, the priest took off his wristwatch and placed it on the lectern alongside the Bible. The boy's grandmother didn't explain this move so the little boy asked, "Granny, what does that mean?" "I'm afraid," said his grandmother, "that doesn't mean a thing."

Great EXPECTATIONS

A visiting preacher was asked to preach a sermon that would attract husbands in the congregation, few of whom were inclined to give up an evening in front of the television to attend the Sunday night service.

Believing a hard-hitting sermon on a motivational theme would bring them in, the preacher decided to preach on the text: "I can do all things through Christ who strengthens me." This was the title he gave to the pastor a week in advance so that it could be advertised in the local newspaper.

Sunday night came and the church was filled to overflowing with a great crowd of men. After the service, several of them approached the preacher with an air of disappointment. "We did appreciate your sermon," said one of the men, "but you didn't keep to your title."

Puzzled, the preacher asked to see the advertisement in the local newspaper and immediately all became clear. Instead of "Ten words to transform your life", the paper's description of his sermon read "Ten words to transform your wife".

Quick Quotes

"Better to light a candle than curse the darkness."

"Doubt is faith knocking at the door asking for admittance."
Bruce Theilman

Gift of
INTERPRETATION

An interpreter in Korea was working with a very famous, but rigid Bible teacher who began his sermon like this: "The theological implications of this text are, to say the least, filled with the deepest and most profound significance."

"He hasn't really said anything worthwhile yet," the interpreter conveyed to the audience, "but when he does I will let you know."

That's RICH

The meanest, yet richest man in town phoned the pastor of a church with this question, "If I left my entire estate to your church, would I go to heaven?" Not wanting to deny his church the benefits of the rich man's estate, the pastor replied cautiously, "I don't think so, but it might be worth a try."

SECRET *Service*

A woman, donating a Communion Table to her local church, impressed upon the pastor her wish for the gift to remain anonymous. But she was greatly troubled when the beautiful carved table was put in place in time for the next Communion service.

"I told you I wanted the gift to be anonymous," she said, taking the pastor aside. "So it is," he replied. "No it's not," she cried. "It says clearly on the front of the table 'In Remembrance of Me'."

Quick Quotes

"*The most important questions we ask of God are the ones that have no answers. This leads to the deepest trust.*"
Larry Crabb

"*Christ went to hell for you because He didn't want to go to heaven without you.*"
General Booth

EMPATHIC
Teaching

A young minister, with very small children, preached to his congregation on the theme "10 Ways to Raise Good and Godly Children". Some years later, with his children entering their teens, he returned to this theme, but the same sermon was now entitled: "10 Suggestions for Raising Good and Godly Children." Several years later still, with his children now in their late teens, the sermon got another airing, this time presented as "Feeble Hints for Fellow Strugglers".

In His OWN *Time*

A man who was praying for help with his finances asked the Lord: "Is it true that with You one day is as a thousand years and a thousand years as one day?" "Yes," said the Lord. "And would it be true that a million dollars is as a few cents, and a few cents as a million dollars?" "Yes", said the Lord. "Then will you give me a million dollars?" requested the man. "Yes", said the Lord, "in a few days."

Quick Quotes

"Coincidences are God's way of remaining anonymous."

"We both believe and disbelieve a hundred times a minute."

"An optimist is someone who, when he hears a preacher say, 'And now, finally ...' , believes him."

Blind FAITH

Two women were discussing the merits and demerits of their respective ministers. "Do you know the colour of your pastor's eyes?" asked one. "No, I never really get a good look at them" said the other, "he closes his eyes when he prays, and when he preaches, I close mine."

Quick Quotes

"*A church is not where a minister leads members but where a minister leads other ministers.*"
Gary Divine

"*Always, always, always – prayer is the most important task we can undertake in any day.*"
Wyndham Hughes

*Amusing Anecdotes
and Quick Quotes*

PEOPLE
& LIFE

Friendly ADVICE

A man went to a psychiatrist with a worrying problem. "Every time I get into bed," he said, "I'm convinced there is someone under it." "I can help," said the psychiatrist, "but it will mean a session a week for a year, costing £30 per visit". The man never returned, so when the psychiatrist met him in the street he asked why he hadn't come back. "Oh, a friend cured me for nothing," he explained. "How?" asked the psychiatrist. "He told me to cut the legs off the bed."

A SHAGGY
Dog Story

Two airport baggage handlers discovered that the small dog in a cage they were unloading from an aircraft was dead. When they heard that the dog belonged to a very old lady who was waiting in the arrival lounge they were moved to compassion, so told the owner that her dog had not arrived on the arranged flight and would be delivered to her home the next day.

The thoughtful men clubbed together and purchased a dog that looked as much like the original as possible, hoping that the owner wouldn't notice any difference.

They took the pup to the old lady's house, but when she looked into the cage and saw the dog eagerly waiting to be released, she exclaimed, "That's not my dog – my dog was dead!"

Concise ADVICE

A man was driving down a narrow country lane when he met a car coming in the opposite direction. Carefully manoeuvring to make way, he was surprised, as he came alongside, to hear the other driver shout out of his window, "Pig!"

Feeling rather wounded, but restraining himself from replying in kind, he drove on pondering what he had done to deserve such an insult. Deep in thought, he turned the next corner and ran straight into a pig.

Quick Quotes

"Humankind cannot bear too much reality."
T S Eliot

"Nothing is impossible until you give it to a committee."

"Life can be understood backwards but it has to be lived forwards."

Hiding on the TELEPHONE

A man telephoned his friend and was surprised when the call was answered on the first ring. A young boy's voice whispered, "Who's there?" "Can I speak to your father?" the man asked. "No," said the small boy quietly, "he's talking to the police." "Well," he said, "can I speak with your mother then?" "No," the child whispered, "she's talking to the firemen."

"What's going on there young man?" the caller demanded. Still in a whisper came the reply, "They are all out looking for me."

MUMMIES *Don't Always Know Best*

An archeologist discovered a mummified figure in the Holy Land and was astonished at how perfect the remains were. His colleagues wondered how the remarkably preserved man had died. "I know how he met his end," the discoverer claimed. "It was a heart attack."

Later, when scientists confirmed that sudden heart failure was indeed the cause of death, the discoverer's colleagues were intrigued to find out how he had come by his verdict, as they knew he had no medical training.

"It was simple," the archeologist revealed, "I found a piece of parchment in his hand on which was written in Hebrew: '100 shekels on Goliath'."

It's in the BAG

Four men were in a small plane; the pilot, a young Boy Scout, a travelling salesman and a man with the reputation of being the smartest man in the world.

Suddenly, something went seriously wrong with the plane and the pilot informed them, "I'm afraid we are going to have to abandon the aircraft. Unfortunately we have only three parachutes. I must have one of them because the airline which employs me insists I save myself so that I can continue to serve them."

Putting on a parachute, the pilot baled out, leaving the other two parachutes on the floor amongst the few items the passengers had brought with them.

"I must have one to save myself because I am so important," said the smartest man in the world and, reaching for a parachute, jumped out of the plane.

"Now what are we going to do?" the travelling salesman groaned, "with only one parachute between us?" "Don't worry," said the Boy Scout cheerily, "the smartest man in the world has just left with my rucksack!"

Quick Quotes

"The mind cannot be chained; it will return time and time again to that which gives it pain."
Sigmund Freud

"The ship drives east, the ship drives west, whatever the gale that blows. 'Tis the set of the sail and not the gale that determines the way she goes."
Elouisa Wilcox

Be Thankful for
SMALL MERCIES

The key speaker at a Yale University graduation ceremony took each letter of the word "Yale" as the basis for his talk. For an hour he tediously explored the topics of Youth, Action, Life, Endeavour.

At the end of his presentation, one member of his bored audience was heard to remark to his neighbour, "I'm sure glad we are not graduating from the Massachusetts Institute of Technology!"

DYING *to Get Away*

The servant of a wealthy merchant was in a Baghdad market securing provisions for his master when he had the most frightful experience of his life. He rushed home to his master and said, "I have just seen Death in the marketplace and he raised his arm as if to strike me. Please, Master, lend me your fastest horse so I can get away."

"Where will you go?" asked his master. "To Samaria," said the servant, "Death will not find me there."

Later the master went to the marketplace himself and also saw Death in the crowd. He asked Death, "Why did you raise your arm to strike my servant?" "I meant him no harm," said Death. "Raising my hand was a gesture of surprise. I didn't expect to find him here, you see, I have an appointment with him tonight, in Samaria."

MOVING *on Up*

A florist was asked to send appropriate flowers to a newly located Bank and also to a funeral. The funeral flowers were meant to have a card attached reading "in deepest sympathy" and the flowers for the Bank a card with a message of good wishes.

Unfortunately, the cards got mixed up and, when he discovered the mistake, the florist rang the Bank first of all to apologise. "Don't let it bother you," said the Bank Manager, "these things happen, but I do just wonder what was said on the card with the funeral flowers.

"Well," said the florist, "I am

rather concerned about the possible reaction when the card is read out at the funeral because the message reads 'Congratulations on your new location!'"

Quick Quotes

"If a way to the better there be, it exacts a full look at the worst."
Thomas Hardy

"It is good to be open-minded, but not so open-minded that your brains fall out."
John Stott

DEAD *Ringer*

A man was shocked one day, on opening his newspaper, to find his name and address printed in the obituary column. He rang a friend to ask whether he had seen his name there. "Yes," said his friend, "I did come across it at the very moment you telephoned." "By the way," he enquired hesitantly, after a pause, "where are you calling from?"

NICE *Paint Work*

An odd-job man knocked on the doors of some wealthy residents, looking for work. At one house he was told, "You can paint the porch. You'll find some paint in the garage." He returned sometime later and said, "I've finished the job you gave me to do, but it wasn't a Porsche – it was a Ferrari."

Quick Quotes

"If I were a doctor and I could prescribe one cure for the modern ills of life it would be silence."
Søren Kierkegaard

"The silliest person in the world is he or she who complains about what they do not have instead of being grateful for what they do have."

AIR *Head*

An novice pilot was flying over London when flight control asked for his height and position. He answered, "I'm 5' 8" and I'm sitting in the cockpit."

The MEASURE
of a Man

A boy's school report put his height at the beginning of the term as 4'6". However at the end of the term his height was recorded as only 4'5". The headmaster's comment beside this note was, "He seems to be settling down nicely."

Low STANDARDS *at High* ALTITUDE

A businessman, travelling on a short flight between Atlanta and Charlotte in the USA, found a cockroach in the meal handed out mid-flight. He complained bitterly to the stewardess who assured him his complaint would be heard at the highest level.

A few days later, he received a very apologetic letter from the president of the airline. Stuck to the back of the letter, however, was an unfortunate note to an airline secretary. It read "Send the usual cockroach letter."

Quick Quotes

"*The difference between winners and losers is that winners do the things losers don't want to do.*"

"*You make a living from what you get. You make a life from what you give.*"

"*Retirement is when the sun rises and you don't have to.*"

From the MOUTHS *of Babes*

Whilst on a hiking trip a university professor lost his way and, on coming across a young boy fishing in a lake, approached him, asking, "Do you know the name of the next town?" "No, I don't," said the boy. "Do you know the name of this long road I am on?" the professor then tried. "Nope," he replied. "You don't know very much, do you?" said the professor, dismayed by the ignorance of this young boy. "No," agreed the child, "but then I am not lost."

Quick Quotes

"Success is choosing your failures carefully."

"Life is 10% of what you make it and 90% of how you take it."
Robert Schuller

"Profanity is the effort of a feeble mind to express itself forcibly."

"Where ID is, let EGO be."
Sigmund Freud's summary of his
theory

*"Some problems are not meant to be
solved; they are meant to be
outgrown."*
Larry Crabb

*"A woman came from a man once –
every other man has come from a
woman."*
John Elder

*"If the only tool a carpenter has is a
hammer he is likely to treat
everything as a nail."*

"Success is when you get what you want. Satisfaction is when you want what you get."

3

*Amusing Anecdotes
and Quick Quotes*

FRIENDS &
RELATIONS

Whose PROBLEM *is it Anyway?*

A man sought his doctor's advice because he was concerned about his wife's apparently increasing deafness.

"Here's how to evaluate it," said the doctor. "Stand about 10 feet away and ask a question in a normal voice. If she doesn't hear, take a step forward and ask it again. Continue to move forward, asking the same question until she responds."

The husband returned home and did just what the doctor suggested. Standing in the kitchen about 10 feet away from his wife, he asked, "What's for lunch today Dear?" Hearing no reply he moved closer and asked the same question again, but still heard no reply. Eventually, he stood just 2 feet away and asked again, "What's for lunch today Dear?"

"I've just told you several times," she replied, "it's vegetable soup. Are you going deaf?"

Quick Quotes

"The best way to get your child's attention is to look comfortable."
Barbara Mysore

"Keep your words soft and sweet just in case you have to eat them."

Love NEVER *Fails*

A surgeon tells of an incident which moved him deeply. His patient, a woman, was left with a slightly crooked lip after surgery to remove a cancerous growth. She awaited her husband's first visit after the removal of the dressing with some dread. Surveying the anxious face as she turned towards him, the husband's immediate response on entering the room was: "Honey, I think it looks cute!" and then, slightly twisting his own lip so that it matched hers, he bent down and tenderly kissed her. The surgeon never forgot the radiance of her smile.

Marriage ADDS *Up*

Two small boys were discussing the subject of marriage. "How many times can people be married?" asked one boy of the other. He thought for a moment and said, "Sixteen times, I think." "How come?" he returned. "Well," said the boy, "in the weddings I have been to, I have heard the pastor say, 'Four better, Four worse, Four richer, Four poorer.' That makes 16, doesn't it?"

Quick Quotes

"Far too many find fault as if there was a reward in it."

"A friend is like blood rushing to a wound without waiting to be called."

Don't RABBIT

A mother, realising that Danny, her children's pet rabbit, was seriously sick, gathered her children together at bedtime and said, "I'm afraid we are going to have get rid of Danny." The children were distraught, far more distressed than she had anticipated and one of them began to cry. Looking around at their shocked faces, she voiced her surprise, "After all," she said, "he is only a rabbit." "Danny?" they chorused, "We thought you said 'Daddy'."

Quick Quote

"*Everything that needs to be said has been said but, as people were not listening, it needs to be said again and again.*"
C S Lewis

IGNORANCE
is not Bliss

A wife complained that her husband did not pay her enough attention. "I do all sorts of things around the house that you are simply not aware of!" she complained. "Like what?" he challenged. "See! I told you!" she said.

Quick Quotes

"When the student is ready the teacher appears."

"We like to forgive and forget as long as the other person doesn't forget that we forgave."

PERFECT
Predecessor

A preacher, describing the human condition, put this question to his congregation: "Is there anyone here who claims to be perfect? If so, stand up." To his surprise, a man at the back of the church got immediately to his feet.

"Do you mean to tell me you are perfect?" asked the pastor. "Oh no," said the man, "I'm far from perfect. I'm standing in for my wife's first husband."

HEAD *to Toe*

When the son of a minister reached driving age, he pleaded with his father to buy him a car. "If you improve your grades in the next year and get your hair cut, I will buy you a car", his father promised. Once his grades improved the boy reminded his father of his promise. "Sure your grades have improved," said his father, "but you haven't cut your hair." "I have thought a lot about that," said the son, "but, as Jesus never cut his hair, I thought I would be like Him and not have mine cut either." "That's fine," said his father, "but remember – Jesus walked!"

Quick Quotes

"For a person who has no forgiveness in his or her heart, living is a worse punishment than death."
Greg Dyson

"Love is moving toward others without self-protection."
Larry Crabb

Rarely HEARD

Things you will rarely hear a man say:
a) Tell me that again, but in a little more detail.
b) You have the wine, I'll drive.
c) Never mind the cost, if you like it, get it.

Things you will rarely hear a woman say:
a) I love your table manners.
b) I wish you wouldn't tell me you love me so often.
c) My feet are lovely and warm.

Sue Devont in *Men and Women*

Quick Quotes

"To travel hopefully is better than to arrive."

"It's better to debate an issue without settling it than settling an issue without debating it."
Bob Monkhouse

"A gossip is someone who talks about others. A bore is someone who talks about himself. A brilliant conversationalist is someone who talks about you."

"Behind every great man is a surprised mother-in-law."

"The mental pain of a breakdown is often the echo of the pain of a long lost relationship."

4

Quotable Comments
about

THE BIBLE
& PRAYER

Quotable Comments

"A thorough knowledge of the Bible is worth more than a college education."
Theodore Roosevelt

"Nobody ever outgrows scripture; the book widens and deepens with our years."
C H Spurgeon

Quotable Comments

"There is medicine in the Bible for every sin-sick soul, but every soul does not need the same medicine."
R A Torrey

"When you have read the Bible you will know that it is the Word of God, because you will have found it the key to your own heart, your own happiness, your own duty."
Woodrow Wilson

Quotable Comments

"The soul can do nothing without the Word of God, and the soul can manage without anything except the Word of God."
Martin Luther

"Knowledge of scripture is knowledge of Christ and ignorance of them is ignorance of him."
Jerome

Quotable Comments

"The scriptures teach us the best way of living, the noblest way of suffering, and the most comfortable way of dying."

John Flavel

Quotable Comments

"We cannot rely on the doctrine of scripture until we are absolutely convinced that God is its author."
John Calvin

"Read all the prophetic books without seeing Christ in them, and what will you find so stupid and flat? See Christ there, and what you read becomes flagrant."
John Chrysostom

Quotable Comments

"No public man in these islands ever believes that the Bible means what it says; he is always convinced that it says what he means."
George Bernard Shaw

Quotable Comments

Most people are bothered by the parts of scripture which they cannot understand; but as for me, I have always noticed that the passages in scripture which trouble me most are those which I do understand."
Mark Twain

Quotable Comments

"*Next to praying there is nothing so important in practical religion as Bible-reading.*"
J C Ryle

"*Our reading of the gospel story can be and should be an act of personal communion with the living Lord.*"
William Temple

Quotable Comments

"We come to a cradle in order to see the baby, so we come to the Bible to see Christ."
Martin Luther

"How petty are the books of the philosophers with all their pomp, compared with the gospels!"
Jean Jaques Rousseau

Quotable Comments

"When I stop praying the coincidences stop happening."
William Temple

"Certain thoughts are prayers. There are moments when whatever be the attitude of the body, the soul is on its knees."
Victor Hugo, *Les Miserables*

Quotable Comments

*"If I had one gift, and only one gift,
to make to the Christian church, I
would offer the gift of prayer."*
E. Stanley Jones

*"You know the price of prayer: it is
precious beyond all price. Never,
never neglect it."*
Thomas Buxton

Quotable Comments

"Prayer is the first thing, the second thing, the third thing necessary to a minister. Pray, then, my dear brother, pray, pray, pray."
Edward Payson

"There is but one road which reaches God and that is prayer; if anyone shows you another, you are being deceived."
Teresa of Avila

Quotable Comments

"Faith is to prayer what the feather
is to the arrow; without prayer it
will not hit the mark."
J C Ryle

"And Satan trembles when he sees
The weakest saint upon his knees."
William Cowper

Quotable Comments

"The best prayers have more often groans than words."
John Bunyan

"You cannot alter the will of God, but the man of prayer can discover God's will."
Sundar Singh

Quotable Comments

"Prayer is the overflowing of the heart in the presence of God."
Madame Guyon, *A Short and Easy Method of Prayer*

"Do not pray for easy lives. Pray to be stronger men. Do not pray for tasks equal to your powers. Pray for powers equal to your tasks."
Phillips Brooks

Quotable Comments

"*I have so much to do that I must spend several hours in prayer before I am able to do it.*"
John Wesley

"*You can't pray a lie.*"
Mark Twain, *The Adventures of Huckleberry Finn*

"*You need not cry very loud: he is nearer to us than we think.*"
Brother Lawrence

Quotable Comments

"I overheard him in prayer, but, good God, with what life and spirit did he pray! It was with so much reverence, as if he were speaking to God, yet with so much confidence as if he were speaking to his friend." Theodorus, writing of Martin Luther

Quotable Comments

"I fear John Knox's prayers more than I fear an army of ten thousand men."
Mary Queen of Scots

"A man who says his prayers in the evening is a captain posting his sentries. After that, he can sleep."
Charles Baudelaire

Quotable Comments

"The first rule of true prayer is to have heart and mind in the right mood for talking with God."
John Calvin

"There is nothing that makes us love a man so much as praying for him."
William Law

Quotable Comments

"*True intercession is a sacrifice, a bleeding sacrifice.*"
J H Jowett

"*Prayer is not merely expressing our present desires. Its purpose is to exercise and train our desires, so that we want what he is getting ready to give us. His gift is very great, and we are small vessels for receiving it. So prayer involves widening our hearts to God.*"
Augustine of Hippo

NATIONAL DISTRIBUTORS

UK: (AND COUNTRIES NOT LISTED BELOW)
CWR, PO Box 230, Farnham, Surrey GU9 8EP.
Tel: (01252) 784710 Outside UK (44) 1252 784710

AUSTRALIA: CMC Australasia, PO Box 519, Belmont, Victoria 3216. Tel: (03) 5241 3288

CANADA: CMC Distribution Ltd, PO Box 7000, Niagara on the Lake, Ontario L0S 1JO. Tel: (0800) 325 1297

GHANA: Challenge Enterprises of Ghana, PO Box 5723, Accra. Tel: (021) 222437/223249 Fax: (021) 226227

HONG KONG: Cross Communications Ltd, 1/F, 562A Nathan Road, Kowloon. Tel: 2780 1188 Fax: 2770 6229

INDIA: Crystal Communications, 10-3-18/4/1, East Marredpally, Secunderabad — 500 026. Tel/Fax: (040) 7732801

KENYA: Keswick Bookshop, PO Box 10242, Nairobi. Tel: (02) 331692/226047

MALAYSIA: Salvation Book Centre (M) Sdn Bhd, 23 Jalan SS 2/64, 47300 Petaling Jaya, Selangor. Tel: (03) 78766411/78766797 Fax: (03) 78757066/78756360

NEW ZEALAND: CMC New Zealand Ltd, Private Bag, 17910 Green Lane, Auckland. Tel: (09) 5249393 Fax: (09) 5222137

NIGERIA: FBFM, Helen Baugh House, 96 St Finbarr's College Road, Akoka, Lagos. Tel: (01) 7747429/4700218/825775/827264

PHILIPPINES: OMF Literature Inc, 776 Boni Avenue, Mandaluyong City. Tel: (02) 531 2183 Fax: (02) 531 1960

REPUBLIC OF IRELAND: Scripture Union, 40 Talbot Street, Dublin 1. Tel: (01) 8363764

SINGAPORE: Campus Crusade Asia Ltd, 315 Outram Road, 06-08 Tan Boon Liat Building, Singapore 169074.
Tel: (065) 222 3640

SOUTH AFRICA: Struik Christian Books, 80 MacKenzie Street, PO Box 1144, Cape Town 8000.
Tel: (021) 462 4360 Fax: (021) 461 3612

SRI LANKA: Christombu Books, 27 Hospital Street, Colombo 1. Tel: (01) 433142/328909

TANZANIA: CLC Christian Book Centre, PO Box 1384, Mkwepu Street, Dar es Salaam. Tel: (051) 2119439

UGANDA: New Day Bookshop, PO Box 2021, Kampala.
Tel: (041) 255377

ZIMBABWE: Word of Life Books, Shop 4, Memorial Building, 35 S Machel Avenue, Harare. Tel: (04) 781305 Fax: (04) 774739

For e-mail addresses, visit the CWR web site: www.cwr.org.uk

My Favourite
£3.99

My Favourite Prayers

A thoughtful collection of prayers of petition and praise concerned with all aspects of the Christian life. An inspiring gift for new Christians as well as for those experienced in the faith.

My Favourite Stories about Children

These charming stories about things that children say and do will amuse and delight your friends and your congregation. A wonderful book that will make you smile and remind you what a blessing children really are.

Tails

Devotional Activity Books: £3.95
Story Books: £4.95

Tails is an exciting series created to help young
children understand the Bible. The books
are written by the award winning
children's author, **Karyn Henley**, and the
characters are created by **Debbie Smith**
who works with the Oscar winning **Wallace
and Gromit**™ team.

Devotional Activity Books
Bible Friends
Learn about great Bible friendships such as
Jonathan and David and Mary and Martha.

Who is Jesus?
Discover the One who is the Son of God,
the Prince of Peace, the Friend and Helper.

Let's Worship
Learn to worship anytime and anywhere,
alone or with others.

Story Books
Friends Forever
No matter how many mistakes we make
true friends always love us.

Who's Whoo-oo-oo?
Jesus is revealed as our best Friend.

Twigs and the Treasure Box
Tails friends discover the greatest treasure
of all.

Pocket Devotionals
£4.99

One-Year devotionals

This attractive series features easy to read selections from Selwyn Hughes' most popular work, **Every Day with Jesus**. The luxurious presentation of these pocket-sized books makes them an inspired gift or travel companion.

Meeting with God

Living with Jesus

Walking in the Spirit

Pocket Encouragers
£3.99

This new series offers biblical help, guidance and encouragement. Each title explores various aspects of the Christian experience, such as relationships, Bible study and coping with responsibility. Some content is common to all titles, with unique material that relates especially to men, women, leaders or young adults. Great gifts!

Pocket Encourager for Men

Pocket Encourager for Women

Pocket Encourager for Leaders

Pocket Encourager for Young Adults